The Data Gold Rush:

Unlocking the Value of Big Data

By

Sandra W. Gray

TABLE OF CONTENTS

Introduction

A. The Growing Importance of Data

In the modern digital age, data has become the lifeblood of our society, reshaping industries, revolutionizing decision-making processes, and unlocking unprecedented opportunities for growth and innovation. The sheer volume of data being generated and collected every day is staggering, and its significance continues to grow exponentially. Welcome to "The Data Gold Rush: Unlocking the Value of Big Data," where we embark on a captivating journey into the world of big data and explore its profound impact on our lives.

With the advent of the internet, social media, mobile devices, and the Internet of Things (IoT), data production has reached an unprecedented scale. Organizations, governments, and individuals are generating colossal amounts of data with every click, swipe, and transaction, resulting in what experts refer to as the "data explosion." This explosion is not just about the quantity of data; it also pertains to the variety and velocity at which data is being generated. From structured information in databases to unstructured content like text, images, and videos, the diversity of data types is astounding.

As businesses and institutions strive to remain competitive and relevant in this data-driven era, the ability to harness the power of big data has become a strategic imperative. Data-driven insights have the potential to unlock previously hidden patterns, trends, and correlations that can drive intelligent decision-making, enhance customer experiences, and optimize processes across diverse sectors. From healthcare and finance to manufacturing and entertainment, data has permeated every aspect of our lives.

However, despite its immense potential, the true value of big data remains largely untapped. In many cases, organizations find themselves overwhelmed by the sheer volume of data at their disposal, struggling to derive meaningful insights from the digital ocean they are navigating. The complexity of data analysis, the need for skilled data scientists, and concerns related to data privacy and security often act as barriers, hindering the full realization of big data's potential.

"The Data Gold Rush: Unlocking the Value of Big Data" seeks to demystify the world of big data and help readers understand how to navigate through this wealth of information effectively. Throughout the book, we will explore the origins of the data gold rush, the fundamental concepts of big data, and the transformative impact it has on businesses and society. We will delve into the strategies employed by pioneering organizations to extract value from data and how data analytics, coupled with the expertise of data scientists, can unearth valuable insights that lead to sustainable success.

This book is not just for data professionals or industry experts; it is for anyone curious about the role of data in our lives and the potential it holds for shaping our collective future. Whether you are a business leader, a student, or an enthusiast eager to understand the data-driven landscape, this book will equip you with the knowledge and insights needed to harness the full potential of big data and thrive in the data gold rush.

Join us on this exciting expedition into the world of data-driven transformation. As we dig deep into the complexities of big data, we will unravel the mysteries, debunk the myths, and equip you with the tools to unlock the true value of data in this era of the data gold rush. The journey begins, and the stakes are high—there's gold in them thar data!

B. The Big Data Revolution

In the last couple of decades, the world has witnessed a seismic shift in the way data is generated, collected, and utilized. The emergence of the internet, coupled with advancements in technology, has given rise to what can only be described as the "Big Data Revolution." Welcome to "The Data Gold Rush: Unlocking the Value of Big Data," where we embark on a captivating journey into this revolutionary era and explore how big data is reshaping the very fabric of our existence.

The Big Data Revolution is a transformational phenomenon that has permeated virtually every aspect of our lives. It refers to the unprecedented scale of data production, storage, and analysis that has taken place in recent years. This revolution is characterized not only by the sheer volume of data being generated but also by its velocity and variety. With the rise of social media platforms, mobile devices, connected gadgets, and sensors, data is now flowing into the digital ecosystem at an astonishing pace. From structured data found in traditional databases to unstructured data like emails, tweets, images, and videos, the diversity of data types is vast and constantly expanding.

At the heart of the Big Data Revolution lies the promise of valuable insights that can drive innovation, optimize processes, and revolutionize decision-making. Organizations and businesses, both large and small, are realizing that data is not merely a byproduct of their operations but a strategic asset that can provide a competitive edge. The ability to harness this data has become a critical determinant of success in today's hyper-competitive landscape.

One of the key drivers of this revolution is the rise of data analytics. Traditional methods of data analysis were ill-equipped to handle the colossal amounts of data being generated daily. However, with the advent of sophisticated data analytics tools and technologies, organizations can now derive meaningful patterns and correlations from massive datasets. Data analytics has empowered businesses to make data-driven decisions, allowing them to understand their customers better, optimize their supply chains, and create personalized experiences.

Moreover, the Big Data Revolution is also fueled by the growing popularity of artificial intelligence (AI) and machine learning (ML). These technologies are not only capable of processing vast amounts of data at unprecedented speeds but also possess the ability to learn from this data and improve their performance over time. AI and ML have opened up new frontiers in fields such as healthcare, finance, autonomous vehicles, and more.

While the Big Data Revolution has unlocked immense opportunities, it has also brought forth new challenges. Data privacy and security have become major concerns as the volume of personal and sensitive data being stored and processed increases. Ethical considerations surrounding data use, such as bias in AI algorithms and potential misuse of data, have also come to the forefront.

"The Data Gold Rush: Unlocking the Value of Big Data" endeavors to shed light on the multifaceted landscape of the Big Data Revolution. Throughout this book, we will explore the origins, evolution, and transformative power of big data. We will delve into the opportunities and challenges it presents, the innovative techniques of data analytics and AI, and the potential implications for society.

Join us on this exhilarating expedition into the heart of the Big Data Revolution. As we traverse the data-rich terrain, we will equip you with the knowledge and insights needed to navigate this transformative era and extract the true value of big data. The journey is thrilling, and the stakes are high—welcome to the data gold rush!

C. The Promise of Unlocking Value

In a world where data has become the new currency, unlocking its hidden value has emerged as the Holy Grail of the digital age. Welcome to "The Data Gold Rush: Unlocking the Value of Big Data," an enlightening exploration of the immense promise that lies within the vast realm of big data and how it has the potential to revolutionize the way we live, work, and interact.

Data, in its raw form, may seem overwhelming, chaotic, and at times insurmountable. However, beneath the surface of this data deluge lies a treasure trove of insights waiting to be discovered. The promise of unlocking value from big data is not just confined to businesses and organizations; it extends to the very core of our society. From transforming industries to improving public services and enhancing individual experiences, the possibilities are as boundless as the data itself.

At the heart of the promise lies the potential for groundbreaking innovation. The wealth of data available today allows us to gain a deeper understanding of our customers, patients, citizens, and the environment. By leveraging data analytics and advanced algorithms, we can identify patterns, forecast trends, and anticipate future needs with unprecedented accuracy. This, in turn, empowers decision-makers to make informed choices that lead to increased efficiency, cost savings, and ultimately a better quality of life for people around the globe.

One of the most significant promises of unlocking value from big data is its potential to revolutionize healthcare. The integration of patient data, combined with AI-driven diagnostics and personalized treatment plans, holds the key to delivering precision medicine. Diseases can be detected at earlier stages, and treatments can be tailored to individual patients, significantly improving health outcomes and saving lives.

Moreover, in the realm of business, data-driven insights have the power to transform traditional industries and pave the way for disruptive innovations. By understanding consumer behavior, companies can offer personalized products and services, creating a seamless and delightful customer experience. Supply chains can be optimized, reducing wastage and environmental impact. Furthermore, predictive analytics can mitigate risks, drive strategic planning, and open up new revenue streams.

Unlocking the value of big data also extends to areas of public interest, such as urban planning and governance. Data-driven smart cities can enhance infrastructure, optimize traffic flow, and improve public services by understanding the needs and preferences of citizens. Additionally, the amalgamation of data from various sources can help governments make well-informed policy decisions that address societal challenges and foster inclusive growth.

However, with great promise comes great responsibility. As we embark on this data-driven journey, it is imperative to address ethical concerns and data privacy issues. Safeguarding sensitive information and ensuring transparent data practices are paramount to building trust and sustaining the value of big data.

"The Data Gold Rush: Unlocking the Value of Big Data" aims to take readers on an enlightening expedition into the untapped potential of big data. Throughout this book, we will navigate the data landscape, unravel its intricacies, and equip readers with the knowledge and tools needed to seize the opportunities presented by the data gold rush. Whether you are a business leader, a policymaker, or a curious individual eager to understand the transformative power of data, this book will be your guide to unlocking the full potential of big data and turning it into a catalyst for positive change.

Join us on this exhilarating quest to unlock the promise of big data. As we journey through the data gold rush, we will reveal the true value that lies within, shaping a future that is not only data-driven but also visionary, inclusive, and brimming with endless possibilities.

Chapter 1
The Origins of the Data Gold Rush

A. From Information Age to Data Age

To comprehend the genesis of the data gold rush, we must first trace the transformative journey from the Information Age to the present-day Data Age. The Information Age, also known as the Computer Age or Digital Age, marked a significant shift in human civilization, characterized by the rapid proliferation of information and the rise of digital technology. It set the stage for the data revolution that was yet to come.

The Information Age dawned with the advent of computers and the internet, which revolutionized the way we processed, shared, and accessed information. It was a time when data started moving from traditional physical formats to digital ones, making it easier to store and transmit vast amounts of information across the globe. The rise of personal computers in the 1970s and 1980s brought computing power to the masses, paving the way for a new era of information sharing and communication.

As the internet gained momentum in the 1990s, the world witnessed a paradigm shift in the way information was disseminated. The emergence of the World Wide Web enabled instantaneous access to an ever-expanding repository of knowledge, heralding an era of connectivity and accessibility. Suddenly, information that was once confined to libraries and archives became available at the click of a button, transcending geographical boundaries and empowering individuals with an unprecedented flow of knowledge.

However, it was in the early 21st century that the Information Age began to transition into the Data Age. With the proliferation of digital devices, social media platforms, and online services, the generation of data reached an exponential crescendo. Every interaction, transaction, and online engagement started generating vast amounts of data, giving birth to what we now refer to as big data.

The Data Age signifies not just the abundance of data but also its strategic significance. Data is no longer merely a byproduct of our digital interactions; it has evolved into a valuable resource that fuels innovation, drives decision-making, and shapes the very fabric of our society. From e-commerce platforms tracking consumer preferences to healthcare systems gathering patient data for personalized treatment plans, data has become the currency of the digital realm.

In this chapter, we will explore the pivotal moments and technological breakthroughs that propelled humanity into the Data Age. We will examine how the rapid digitization of information laid the foundation for the data gold rush we are currently experiencing. As we delve deeper into the historical context, we will gain a profound understanding of the factors that triggered the data revolution and how it has transformed the way we perceive and interact with information.

The shift from the Information Age to the Data Age marks a defining moment in human history, as it sets the stage for a future defined by data-driven insights and boundless possibilities. Join us on this illuminating journey through time, as we unravel the origins of the data gold rush and uncover the remarkable evolution from an age of information to an era where data reigns supreme. The story of the data gold rush begins here, with the emergence of the Data Age.

B. Pioneers in Data Utilization

As the Data Age unfolded, a new breed of trailblazers emerged, harnessing the power of data to transform industries, drive innovation, and pioneer new frontiers of knowledge. These visionaries became the pioneers in data utilization, and their groundbreaking efforts laid the groundwork for the data gold rush we witness today.

One of the early pioneers in data utilization was Amazon, the e-commerce giant founded by Jeff Bezos in 1994. From its inception, Amazon recognized the immense value of data in understanding customer behavior and preferences. The company's data-driven approach led to the development of sophisticated algorithms that personalized product recommendations and streamlined the online shopping experience. Through data analytics, Amazon transformed the retail landscape and set a precedent for data-driven businesses across industries.

In the early 2000s, Google emerged as another key pioneer in data utilization. Its founders, Larry Page and Sergey Brin, realized that the vast amounts of data generated from internet searches could be harnessed to deliver more relevant and accurate search results. The PageRank algorithm, based on data analysis and link analysis, revolutionized web search and catapulted Google to become the dominant search engine. Google's data-driven approach extended beyond search to advertising, maps, and numerous other services, solidifying its position as a leading tech giant.

The healthcare industry also witnessed pioneering efforts in data utilization, with companies like IBM Watson Health leading the charge. IBM Watson, an AI-powered cognitive computing system, demonstrated the potential of data analytics in diagnosing and treating complex medical conditions. By analyzing vast amounts of medical literature, research papers, and patient data, Watson could provide insights to healthcare professionals, leading to more accurate diagnoses and personalized treatment plans.

In the realm of social media, Facebook emerged as a data utilization pioneer, capitalizing on the vast troves of user-generated data. With billions of users sharing information and engaging with content daily, Facebook employed data analytics to deliver tailored content and targeted advertisements, creating a highly engaging platform. This data-driven approach not only fueled Facebook's growth but also transformed the way people interact and communicate online.

Beyond the corporate world, the field of scientific research also witnessed pioneering data utilization efforts. The Human Genome Project, completed in 2003, was a landmark achievement in genomics and biology. By deciphering the human genome, researchers produced massive amounts of genetic data that opened new avenues for understanding human health and disease. This project laid the groundwork for personalized medicine and has since driven significant advancements in medical research and treatments.

The pioneers in data utilization recognized that data was not simply an asset to be collected and stored, but a strategic resource that could fuel transformative change. Their innovative use of data analytics, machine learning, and artificial intelligence paved the way for a new era of data-driven decision-making and created a blueprint for future data initiatives.

In this chapter, we will delve into the remarkable contributions of these data pioneers, exploring their groundbreaking achievements and the impact of their data-driven approaches on their respective industries. Through their stories, we will gain valuable insights into the early stages of the data gold rush and how these pioneers laid the foundation for the data-driven world we inhabit today. Their visionary spirit and bold experimentation set the stage for the exciting journey ahead as we continue to unlock the value of big data in "The Data Gold Rush."

C. The Rise of Big Data

In the landscape of the Data Age, the rise of big data has been nothing short of a revolution. The confluence of technological advancements, the exponential growth of digital information, and the increasing demand for data-driven insights laid the foundation for what would become the data gold rush.

The journey of big data's rise can be traced back to the early 2000s when businesses and organizations started grappling with an unprecedented influx of digital information. Traditional databases and data management systems were ill-equipped to handle the sheer volume and variety of data being generated. This marked the beginning of a paradigm shift that would forever alter the way data was collected, stored, and analyzed.

One of the critical enablers of big data's rise was the evolution of data storage and processing technologies. The advent of cloud computing provided scalable and cost-effective solutions to handle vast amounts of data. Cloud storage allowed businesses to store and access data without investing in expensive infrastructure, democratizing data access and unleashing its potential to a broader audience.

Simultaneously, the proliferation of internet-enabled devices such as smartphones, IoT sensors, and wearable gadgets accelerated the generation of data on an unprecedented scale. Each interaction, transaction, and communication contributed to the data deluge that became the hallmark of the Data Age. The explosion of social media platforms further fueled the rise of big data, as billions of users shared their thoughts, opinions, and preferences online, generating a treasure trove of user-generated content.

The concept of the "4 V's" of big data emerged to describe its defining characteristics: Volume, Velocity, Variety, and Veracity. Volume refers to the massive amounts of data being generated every second. Velocity describes the speed at which data is created, collected, and processed. Variety signifies the diverse types of data, including structured, unstructured, and semi-structured data. Lastly, Veracity addresses the challenges of ensuring data accuracy, reliability, and trustworthiness.

With the realization that data could be an invaluable asset, businesses began recognizing the potential for data-driven decision-making. Data analytics emerged as a critical discipline, enabling organizations to extract valuable insights from vast datasets. The development of sophisticated data analytics tools and algorithms allowed businesses to identify patterns, trends, and correlations in the data, enabling more informed and strategic choices.

The rise of big data also marked a paradigm shift in various industries. In finance, data-driven algorithms transformed the way stocks were traded, and risk assessments were made. In healthcare, electronic health records and medical data analytics revolutionized patient care and medical research. In marketing, personalized advertisements based on user behavior became the norm, boosting engagement and conversion rates.

As the demand for big data expertise grew, the role of data scientists and data engineers became increasingly critical. These professionals possessed the skills to wrangle, process, and analyze data effectively, making sense of the immense information influx.

In this chapter, we will explore the pivotal moments and driving forces that catapulted big data into the spotlight. We will delve into the challenges and opportunities presented by the rise of big data and how it has set the stage for the data gold rush we experience today. The exponential growth of data has transformed our world, unlocking a vast ocean of potential waiting to be discovered, analyzed, and harnessed. Join us as we navigate the rise of big data and uncover its transformative power in shaping the data-driven future that awaits us in "The Data Gold Rush."

Chapter 2
Understanding Big Data

A. Defining Big Data

In the era of the data gold rush, the term "Big Data" has become ubiquitous, but what exactly does it entail? Defining Big Data is the crucial first step in comprehending its impact and potential. At its core, Big Data refers to datasets of such immense volume, complexity, and speed that traditional data processing techniques are inadequate to handle them effectively.

The essence of Big Data lies in its sheer magnitude. It encompasses vast amounts of information generated from diverse sources, including social media, online transactions, scientific research, sensor networks, and more. These datasets can reach terabytes, petabytes, or even exabytes in size, dwarfing the data volumes of the past. The proliferation of connected devices and the Internet of Things (IoT) has further contributed to the exponential growth of Big Data.

However, size alone does not define Big Data. It is also characterized by the variety of data it encompasses. Traditional data was typically structured and neatly organized in databases. In contrast, Big Data comprises structured, unstructured, and semi-structured data. This diverse mix includes text documents, images, videos, audio files, social media posts, geospatial data, and sensor readings. The challenge lies in managing and analyzing this disparate data landscape effectively.

Velocity is another defining aspect of Big Data. The data is generated and updated at unprecedented speeds, often in real-time. Social media posts, stock market data, website clicks, and IoT sensor data are just a few examples of data that is streaming in constantly and rapidly. To gain meaningful insights, data must be processed and analyzed in near real-time, necessitating specialized tools and technologies.

Veracity is a critical consideration in the context of Big Data. It refers to the accuracy and reliability of the data. With the massive influx of data from various sources, ensuring the veracity of information becomes a challenge. Data may contain errors, duplicates, inconsistencies, or biases, which can lead to inaccurate analyses and flawed decision-making. As such, data quality and data governance are essential aspects of dealing with Big Data.

While the 4 V's (Volume, Variety, Velocity, Veracity) are widely accepted as defining characteristics of Big Data, there is another emerging V: Value. The true value of Big Data lies in its potential to deliver actionable insights and drive informed decision-making. Organizations that can effectively extract value from Big Data gain a competitive advantage, optimize operations, enhance customer experiences, and identify new business opportunities.

To make sense of Big Data, advanced analytics and data processing techniques are required. Data scientists and analysts employ machine learning algorithms, data mining, natural language processing, and other techniques to identify patterns, correlations, and trends within the vast datasets. Data visualization tools also play a crucial role in presenting complex information in a digestible and intuitive manner.

In this chapter, we will delve deeper into the essence of Big Data, understanding its defining characteristics and the challenges and opportunities it presents. By grasping the intricacies of Big Data, we equip ourselves to navigate the data gold rush effectively, transforming information into actionable insights and unlocking the true value of the digital age's most valuable commodity. Join us as we explore the foundations of Big Data and embark on an illuminating journey to understand its immense significance in "The Data Gold Rush."

B. The 4 V's of Big Data (Volume, Velocity, Variety, Veracity)

In the data-driven landscape of the Data Age, the 4 V's of Big Data—Volume, Velocity, Variety, and Veracity—form the foundation upon which the data gold rush is built. Understanding these defining characteristics is essential to grasping the magnitude and complexity of Big Data and unlocking its true potential.

❖ Volume: Volume refers to the sheer scale of data being generated and collected. Unlike the data volumes of the past, which were relatively modest, Big Data encompasses vast amounts of information on an unprecedented scale. Terabytes, petabytes, and exabytes of data are becoming increasingly common in today's digital ecosystem. The explosion of internet usage, social media interactions, online transactions, IoT sensors, and scientific research have all contributed to the exponential growth of data volume. Organizations now face the challenge of efficiently storing, managing, and analyzing these colossal datasets.

❖ Velocity: Velocity represents the speed at which data is generated and updated. In the era of real-time information, Big Data is in constant motion. From social media posts and website clicks to sensor readings and financial transactions, data streams in rapidly and incessantly. To extract timely and actionable insights from Big Data, traditional batch processing methods are inadequate. Data must be processed and analyzed in near real-time to seize opportunities, mitigate risks, and respond to dynamic changes. The need for sophisticated data processing technologies is crucial to cope with the velocity of Big Data.

❖ Variety: Variety pertains to the diverse types of data present in Big Data. In the past, data was predominantly structured and neatly organized in relational databases. However, with the rise of Big Data, the data landscape has expanded to include structured, unstructured, and semi-structured data. This diverse mix comprises text, images, videos, audio files, social media posts, geospatial data, and more. Each data type requires specialized processing techniques and presents unique challenges for analysis and integration. Effectively managing the variety of data is vital to harness its full potential.

❖ Veracity: Veracity refers to the accuracy and reliability of the data. In the vast ocean of Big Data, ensuring the trustworthiness of information becomes a critical concern. Data may be riddled with errors, duplicates, inconsistencies, or biases, which can significantly impact the outcomes of data analysis and decision-making. As such, maintaining data quality and establishing robust data governance practices are imperative to mitigate the risks associated with veracity. Ensuring data veracity builds confidence in the insights derived from Big Data.

The 4 V's of Big Data encapsulate the fundamental challenges and opportunities that accompany the data gold rush. As organizations strive to capitalize on the potential of Big Data, they must address the complexities of managing large volumes of data, processing it at high speeds, handling diverse data types, and ensuring data accuracy and reliability.

In this chapter, we will delve deeper into each of the 4 V's, exploring their significance and impact on Big Data analytics and decision-making. By understanding these core aspects, readers will gain valuable insights into the multifaceted nature of Big Data and how to navigate the data gold rush effectively. Join us on this enlightening journey to comprehend the 4 V's of Big Data and unlock the true potential of this invaluable resource in "The Data Gold Rush."

C. Challenges and Opportunities

As the data gold rush gains momentum, understanding the challenges and opportunities posed by Big Data is paramount to successfully navigating this transformative era. The very essence of Big Data—its immense volume, velocity, variety, and veracity—gives rise to a host of complexities and possibilities that shape the landscape of data-driven decision-making.

Challenges:

❖ Storage and Infrastructure: Dealing with the vast volume of data requires robust and scalable storage solutions. Traditional databases may struggle to handle the scale of Big Data, necessitating the adoption of distributed file systems and cloud-based storage. Ensuring data accessibility, security, and cost-effectiveness in storage infrastructure is a significant challenge.

❖ Data Quality: Big Data from various sources can be heterogeneous and often contains errors, inconsistencies, and duplicates. Poor data quality can lead to inaccurate analyses and flawed decision-making. Ensuring data cleanliness and quality control are essential to derive meaningful insights from Big Data.

❖ Data Integration: The variety of data types in Big Data poses integration challenges. Combining structured, unstructured, and semi-structured data from disparate sources requires sophisticated data integration techniques. Organizations must invest in tools and methodologies that facilitate seamless data integration.

❖ Real-time Processing: The velocity of Big Data demands real-time or near-real-time processing capabilities. Traditional batch processing may not suffice for time-sensitive insights. Implementing stream processing and real-time analytics becomes critical in capturing valuable opportunities swiftly.

❖ Data Privacy and Security: The vast amount of data collected raises significant concerns about data privacy and security. Organizations must adhere to stringent data protection regulations to safeguard sensitive information and earn the trust of their customers and users.

Opportunities:

❖ Data-Driven Decision Making: Big Data presents a wealth of opportunities for organizations to make data-driven decisions. The ability to analyze vast datasets enables businesses to gain a deeper understanding of customer behavior, optimize operations, and innovate new products and services.

❖ Personalization: With Big Data, organizations can offer personalized experiences to customers. Tailoring products, services, and marketing campaigns based on individual preferences fosters customer loyalty and enhances user satisfaction.

❖ Predictive Analytics: Big Data analytics allows organizations to predict future trends and outcomes with a higher degree of accuracy. Predictive models aid in forecasting demand, identifying potential risks, and making proactive decisions.

❖ Innovation and Research: Big Data opens up new frontiers for scientific research and innovation. In fields like genomics, climate science, and space exploration, Big Data analysis leads to groundbreaking discoveries and advancements.

❖ Improved Public Services: Governments can leverage Big Data to enhance public services, optimize urban planning, and make data-driven policy decisions. Smart cities, traffic management systems, and public health initiatives are just some examples of the positive impact of Big Data on public services.

In this chapter, we will explore in-depth the challenges that organizations face in dealing with Big Data and the strategies they can employ to overcome them. Additionally, we will delve into the vast opportunities that Big Data presents, propelling businesses and society into a future powered by data-driven insights. By understanding the intricacies of Big Data challenges and opportunities, readers will be better equipped to seize the full potential of this invaluable resource in "The Data Gold Rush." Join us on this enlightening journey as we uncover the transformative power of Big Data and its profound implications for the data-driven world.

Chapter 3
Mining Data: Collecting and Storing

A. Data Collection Methods

In the digital age of the data gold rush, data collection has become the cornerstone of acquiring valuable insights and driving informed decision-making. The process of gathering data from various sources is fundamental to unlocking the potential of Big Data. In this chapter, we will explore the diverse data collection methods used to amass vast datasets that fuel the data-driven revolution.

- ❖ Surveys and Questionnaires: Surveys and questionnaires are classic data collection tools used to gather information directly from individuals. Whether conducted in person, via phone calls, or online, surveys allow researchers to obtain structured data on preferences, opinions, and behaviors. With the advent of online survey platforms, data collection has become more accessible and scalable.

❖ Web Scraping: Web scraping involves automatically extracting data from websites. By parsing HTML and other web page elements, organizations can collect information from multiple sources simultaneously. Web scraping enables businesses to track competitors, monitor market trends, and aggregate data from various online platforms.

❖ Social Media Monitoring: Social media has become a treasure trove of valuable data. Social media monitoring tools capture and analyze user-generated content, including posts, comments, and interactions. This data provides organizations with insights into consumer sentiment, brand perception, and emerging trends.

❖ IoT Sensors: The Internet of Things (IoT) is revolutionizing data collection. IoT sensors embedded in devices and machines generate real-time data on environmental conditions, usage patterns, and performance metrics. This data is invaluable in industries like manufacturing, logistics, and environmental monitoring.

❖ Mobile Apps and Wearables: Mobile apps and wearables collect data on users' activities, health, and location. From fitness trackers to smartwatches, wearable devices capture biometric data, allowing individuals and healthcare providers to monitor health and wellness trends.

❖ Transactional Data: Businesses generate large volumes of data through transactions, such as sales records, financial transactions, and customer interactions. These data are often structured and stored in databases, providing valuable insights into business operations and customer behavior.

❖ Machine Data: Machines and devices generate data logs that capture their operational status and performance metrics. This machine-generated data is critical in industries like manufacturing, aviation, and IT, where predictive maintenance and fault detection are essential.

❖ Government Data: Government agencies collect and publish vast amounts of data on demographics, economics, public health, and more. Open data initiatives provide access to public datasets, enabling researchers and businesses to leverage this information for analysis and insights.

❖ Crowdsourcing: Crowdsourcing involves sourcing data from a large group of individuals or contributors. Crowdsourced data can include reviews, ratings, annotations, or even creative contributions. Crowdsourcing is commonly used for data labeling in machine learning applications.

Data collection methods must consider data privacy and ethical considerations. Organizations must adhere to data protection regulations and ensure that data collection processes are transparent and compliant with privacy laws.

In this chapter, we will delve into each data collection method, exploring their strengths, limitations, and applications. Understanding the various data collection approaches empowers organizations to assemble comprehensive datasets and embark on an enriching journey of data mining, analysis, and unlocking the true value of Big Data in "The Data Gold Rush." Join us as we explore the intricacies of data collection and learn how to harness the power of diverse data sources to drive data-driven success.

B. Data Storage and Infrastructure

As data collection continues to soar in the data gold rush era, the challenge of effectively storing and managing the vast volumes of data has become paramount. In this chapter, we delve into the world of data storage and explore the infrastructure required to harness the potential of Big Data effectively.

- ❖ Traditional Databases: Traditional relational databases have been the backbone of data storage for many years. These databases use structured query language (SQL) to manage and retrieve data stored in tables with predefined schemas. While they are suitable for structured data, they may struggle to handle the massive scale and variety of unstructured and semi-structured data associated with Big Data.

❖ Distributed File Systems: In response to the limitations of traditional databases, distributed file systems have emerged as a powerful solution for Big Data storage. Distributed file systems, like Hadoop Distributed File System (HDFS), divide data into blocks and distribute them across multiple nodes in a cluster. This distributed approach allows for high availability, fault tolerance, and scalability, making them ideal for handling vast volumes of data.

❖ NoSQL Databases: NoSQL (Not Only SQL) databases provide a flexible and scalable alternative to traditional databases. Unlike relational databases, NoSQL databases can accommodate unstructured and semi-structured data and support horizontal scaling across multiple servers. Popular NoSQL databases include MongoDB, Cassandra, and Amazon DynamoDB.

❖ Cloud Storage: Cloud computing has revolutionized data storage by providing scalable and cost-effective solutions. Cloud storage services like Amazon S3, Microsoft Azure Blob Storage, and Google Cloud

Storage offer virtually unlimited capacity, pay-as-you-go pricing, and seamless integration with other cloud-based services.

❖ Data Warehouses: Data warehouses are specialized databases designed for analytical processing. They consolidate data from various sources, enabling organizations to perform complex queries and generate business intelligence insights. Data warehouses facilitate data transformation, aggregation, and historical analysis.

❖ In-Memory Databases: In-memory databases store data in main memory, allowing for rapid data retrieval and processing. These databases are particularly useful for real-time analytics and applications that require low-latency access to data.

❖ Object Storage: Object storage systems organize data as objects with unique identifiers and metadata. Object storage is ideal for unstructured data, such as images, videos, and documents. It provides seamless scalability and is commonly used in cloud storage services.

❖ Data Lakes: Data lakes are repositories that store raw, unprocessed data from various sources. They allow organizations to store data in its native format and analyze it later. Data lakes are valuable for exploratory data analysis and machine learning applications.

To ensure data accessibility, reliability, and security, organizations must consider data backup and disaster recovery strategies. Regular data backups protect against data loss, and disaster recovery plans help organizations recover data in case of unforeseen events.

Selecting the appropriate data storage infrastructure depends on factors such as data volume, data type, data access requirements, and budget considerations. Organizations must strike a balance between performance, scalability, and cost-effectiveness.

In this chapter, we explore the diverse data storage options available to organizations and delve into the considerations for selecting the most suitable infrastructure for their Big Data needs. By understanding data storage and infrastructure, organizations can lay a solid foundation for effective data mining, analysis, and unlocking the true potential of Big Data in "The Data Gold Rush." Join us on this enlightening journey as we explore the intricacies of data storage and learn how to build a robust data infrastructure for data-driven success.

C. Ensuring Data Security and Privacy

In the data gold rush era, as organizations amass vast troves of valuable data, ensuring data security and privacy has become a paramount concern. With the proliferation of data breaches and privacy violations, safeguarding sensitive information has become an ethical and legal imperative. In this chapter, we explore the critical aspects of data security and privacy to maintain the trust and confidence of stakeholders.

❖ Encryption: Encryption is a fundamental technique used to protect data from unauthorized access. It involves converting data into a coded format using cryptographic algorithms. Only authorized parties with the appropriate decryption keys can access and read the encrypted data. Data at rest (stored data) and data in transit (data being transmitted over networks) must be encrypted to prevent unauthorized interception and access.

❖ Access Control: Implementing robust access control mechanisms is essential to restrict data access to authorized users only. Organizations can use role-based access control (RBAC) to assign specific privileges to users based on their roles and responsibilities. Multi-factor authentication (MFA) adds an extra layer of security by requiring users to provide additional verification beyond passwords.

❖ Data Masking: Data masking is a technique used to anonymize sensitive data while preserving its format and utility for development, testing, or analytical purposes. By replacing sensitive information with fictitious or obfuscated values, organizations can minimize the risk of exposing sensitive data during non-production use.

❖ Data Governance: Data governance encompasses the processes, policies, and guidelines that ensure the appropriate handling, usage, and protection of data. Establishing data governance frameworks helps organizations maintain data quality, compliance, and security throughout the data lifecycle.

❖ Regular Auditing and Monitoring: Continuous monitoring and auditing of data access and usage are vital to detect potential security breaches or suspicious activities. Monitoring tools and anomaly detection techniques help identify and respond to security incidents promptly.

❖ Privacy by Design: Privacy by Design is an approach that embeds privacy and security measures into the design and development of systems and processes. By proactively addressing privacy concerns from the outset, organizations can ensure that data protection is an integral part of their operations.

❖ Compliance with Data Regulations: Organizations must adhere to relevant data protection regulations, such as the General Data Protection Regulation (GDPR) and the California Consumer Privacy Act (CCPA). Compliance with these regulations ensures that data subjects' rights are protected and that organizations fulfill their legal obligations.

❖ Secure Data Disposal: Proper data disposal is crucial to prevent data leakage. Organizations must establish procedures for securely deleting or destroying data that is no longer needed or has exceeded its retention period.

❖ Employee Training and Awareness: Data security and privacy are not solely technological issues; they also rely on employees' awareness and adherence to security policies. Regular training and education on data security best practices help foster a culture of data protection within the organization.

By adopting a comprehensive approach to data security and privacy, organizations can build trust with their customers and stakeholders and safeguard their valuable data assets. Maintaining a robust security posture not only protects against potential threats but also allows organizations to confidently leverage the full potential of Big Data in the data-driven landscape.

In this chapter, we explore the essential practices and principles that underpin data security and privacy. By understanding the importance of safeguarding data and implementing stringent security measures, organizations can ensure a secure and ethical data mining process in "The Data Gold Rush." Join us on this enlightening journey as we explore the intricacies of data security and privacy and learn how to safeguard valuable data in the dynamic era of Big Data.

Chapter 4
Data is the New Gold: Valuing Data Assets

A. Recognizing Data as an Asset

In the data gold rush, data has emerged as the new currency of the digital era. Organizations worldwide are waking up to the realization that data is not merely a byproduct of operations but a strategic asset that holds immense value. In this chapter, we delve into the significance of recognizing data as a valuable asset and understanding its transformative potential.

Data is the lifeblood of modern businesses, driving innovation, enhancing decision-making, and fueling competitive advantage. As technology continues to advance and data volumes grow exponentially, organizations are coming to understand that data is no longer a commodity to be taken for granted but a resource to be carefully cultivated and managed.

Recognizing data as an asset entails understanding its multifaceted value:

❖ Business Insights: Data provides invaluable insights into customer behavior, market trends, and operational performance. Organizations can leverage these insights to identify growth opportunities, optimize processes, and stay ahead of competitors.

❖ Personalization and Customer Experience: Data enables organizations to offer personalized experiences to customers, tailoring products and services to individual preferences. This enhances customer satisfaction, loyalty, and engagement.

❖ Strategic Decision Making: Data-driven decision-making empowers leaders to base their strategies on concrete evidence rather than intuition. Data analysis helps mitigate risks, validate assumptions, and make informed choices.

❖ Monetization Opportunities: Data itself can be a revenue stream. Organizations can monetize data through data-as-a-service (DaaS) offerings, selling anonymized datasets, or providing valuable insights to external parties.

❖ Data-Driven Innovation: Data fuels innovation and fosters a culture of experimentation. By analyzing data, organizations can identify emerging trends, disruptive technologies, and new product opportunities.

❖ Competitive Advantage: In today's data-centric landscape, organizations that can harness data effectively gain a significant competitive advantage. Data-driven organizations are better equipped to adapt to market changes and respond to customer needs.

To realize the full potential of data as an asset, organizations must adopt a data-driven culture that permeates every level of the organization. This entails:

- Data Governance: Establishing data governance frameworks to ensure data quality, privacy, and compliance.

- Data Literacy: Promoting data literacy among employees, empowering them to interpret and use data effectively.

- Data Integration: Integrating data from various sources to create a comprehensive view of the business landscape.

- Data Monetization: Exploring opportunities to monetize data assets responsibly and ethically.

Recognizing data as an asset also involves treating it with the same level of care and protection as other valuable assets. Organizations must prioritize data security, implement access controls, and enforce data privacy measures to safeguard data integrity and maintain stakeholder trust.

In this chapter, we explore the paradigm shift in how organizations perceive and value data. By understanding the multifaceted nature of data as an asset, readers will gain insights into how data is driving a transformative wave in the data gold rush. Join us on this enlightening journey as we explore the power of data as the new gold and its profound impact on the digital landscape of the future.

B. Data Monetization Strategies

In the data gold rush, organizations are increasingly recognizing the untapped potential of data monetization. Data, once considered a cost center, is now becoming a lucrative revenue stream. In this chapter, we explore the diverse data monetization strategies that empower organizations to unlock the true value of their data assets.

- ❖ Data-as-a-Service (DaaS): DaaS is a model where organizations offer access to their data to external parties for a fee. This can include raw data, enriched datasets, or data APIs. Businesses can package their data into valuable insights, market research, or industry reports, catering to the needs of various customers.

- ❖ Personalized Recommendations: E-commerce and media companies often leverage customer data to provide personalized recommendations to users. By analyzing user behavior and preferences, organizations can offer tailored product recommendations, content suggestions, and advertisements that improve engagement and conversion rates.

❖ Targeted Advertising: Data-driven advertising enables organizations to deliver highly targeted advertisements to specific audience segments. By leveraging user data, advertisers can reach the right audience with relevant ads, maximizing the return on advertising investments.

❖ Data Partnerships and Exchanges: Data partnerships allow organizations to pool and share data with other entities to gain new insights and enrich their datasets. Data exchanges provide platforms where organizations can buy or sell data, fostering a data ecosystem that benefits multiple stakeholders.

❖ Subscription-Based Data Access: Organizations can offer subscription-based access to premium datasets or data analytics tools. Subscribers gain regular access to updated and curated data that adds value to their business operations or research.

❖ Insights for Research and Innovation: Research institutions and businesses can monetize data by providing insights and datasets to fuel scientific research, innovation, and product development. Such collaborations lead to new discoveries and breakthroughs that benefit society as a whole.

❖ IoT Data Monetization: Organizations with IoT deployments can monetize the data generated by IoT devices. By aggregating and analyzing sensor data, organizations can offer predictive maintenance services, optimize supply chains, and deliver valuable insights to customers.

❖ Data Crowdsourcing: Crowdsourced data collection can generate valuable datasets for research or commercial purposes. Organizations can incentivize contributors to share data or insights, which can be further monetized in various applications.

❖ Data-Driven Consultancy: Organizations with specialized expertise in data analysis can offer data-driven consultancy services to other businesses. By providing valuable insights and actionable recommendations, data-driven consultancies add substantial value to client operations.

It is essential for organizations to approach data monetization responsibly and ethically. Respecting data privacy, obtaining explicit consent from data subjects, and adhering to data protection regulations are critical to building trust with customers and stakeholders.

Data monetization requires a strategic approach, understanding the unique value of the data assets, and identifying the most suitable monetization methods for the organization. It involves aligning data monetization strategies with business goals and customer needs.

In this chapter, we delve into the world of data monetization, exploring the strategies that empower organizations to transform data from a valuable asset into a revenue-generating resource. By understanding the breadth of data monetization opportunities, readers will be equipped to capitalize on the immense potential of their data assets in "The Data Gold Rush." Join us on this enlightening journey as we explore the power of data monetization and its impact on shaping the data-driven future.

C. Evaluating the Worth of Data

In the data gold rush, understanding the true worth of data assets is essential for organizations seeking to capitalize on the data-driven revolution. The value of data extends far beyond its sheer volume or variety; it lies in its potential to drive insights, innovations, and informed decision-making. In this chapter, we explore the methodologies and considerations for evaluating the worth of data assets.

- ❖ Business Relevance: The value of data is closely tied to its relevance to the organization's core business objectives. Data that directly impacts revenue generation, customer satisfaction, or operational efficiency holds significant worth. Evaluating how data aligns with strategic goals helps prioritize data assets.

❖ Data Accuracy and Quality: Accurate and high-quality data is more valuable than raw, unverified data. Ensuring data accuracy and reliability is crucial for deriving meaningful insights and making reliable decisions. Data cleansing and validation processes contribute to enhancing the worth of data.

❖ Unique Insights: Data that offers unique insights not available elsewhere is highly valuable. Proprietary data, niche datasets, or data collected from exclusive sources can provide a competitive edge and present monetization opportunities.

❖ Actionable Intelligence: The worth of data lies in its ability to provide actionable intelligence. Data that leads to concrete actions and tangible outcomes is more valuable than data that merely offers general trends or correlations.

❖ Timeliness: Real-time or near-real-time data has higher worth, particularly in dynamic industries where rapid decision-making is critical. Timely insights enable organizations to respond swiftly to changing market conditions.

❖ Potential Impact: Data with the potential to drive significant impact on the organization's performance and profitability is highly valuable. Evaluating the potential return on investment (ROI) of data assets helps gauge their worth.

❖ Data Diversity: A diverse dataset that includes a wide range of variables and attributes can lead to comprehensive insights and robust analyses. The more comprehensive the data, the higher its value in understanding complex scenarios.

❖ Monetization Opportunities: Data that offers multiple avenues for monetization, such as through subscriptions, partnerships, or commercialization, holds considerable worth. Assessing the potential revenue streams from data assets helps in valuation.

❖ Ethical Considerations: Ethical data practices and data privacy are essential factors in determining the worth of data. Compliance with data protection regulations and maintaining customer trust are crucial for unlocking data's full potential.

❖ Future Scalability: Evaluating data assets' scalability and potential to handle future growth is essential. Scalable data assets can accommodate increasing data volumes and retain their value over time.

To evaluate the worth of data accurately, organizations can utilize various analytical techniques, including data valuation models and cost-benefit analysis. Data valuation models assess data based on its utility, rarity, demand, and exclusivity. Cost-benefit analysis helps quantify the potential benefits and associated costs of data assets.

As the data gold rush continues, organizations must continuously reassess and reevaluate the worth of their data assets. The value of data evolves with changing business needs, technological advancements, and market dynamics.

In this chapter, we explore the methodologies for evaluating the worth of data assets and understanding how data's intrinsic value contributes to the data-driven revolution. By grasping the multifaceted nature of data valuation, readers will be equipped to unlock the true potential of their data assets in "The Data Gold Rush." Join us on this enlightening journey as we explore the power of data valuation and its profound impact on shaping the data-driven future.

Chapter 5
Analyzing for Nuggets: Data Analytics

A. Introduction to Data Analytics

In the data gold rush, data analytics has emerged as the key to unlocking the hidden treasures buried within the vast datasets. The ability to extract valuable insights, patterns, and trends from data empowers organizations to make informed decisions and gain a competitive advantage. In this chapter, we delve into the fascinating world of data analytics, exploring its significance, methodologies, and transformative potential.

Data analytics is the process of examining, cleaning, transforming, and modeling data to uncover meaningful information and draw conclusions. It goes beyond merely collecting and storing data; it involves extracting knowledge that can drive actions and create value.

Data analytics encompasses a spectrum of techniques, each serving different purposes:

❖ Descriptive Analytics: Descriptive analytics involves summarizing historical data to understand past events and patterns. It answers the question "What happened?" and provides a retrospective view of business performance. Dashboards, scorecards, and key performance indicators (KPIs) are common tools for descriptive analytics.

❖ Diagnostic Analytics: Diagnostic analytics delves deeper into data to identify the reasons behind past events or trends. It answers the question "Why did it happen?" by analyzing relationships between variables and root causes of specific outcomes.

❖ Predictive Analytics: Predictive analytics employs statistical and machine learning techniques to forecast future outcomes based on historical data. It answers the question "What is likely to happen?" by developing models that anticipate trends and events.

❖ Prescriptive Analytics: Prescriptive analytics takes data analysis a step further by recommending optimal actions based on predictions. It answers the question "What should we do?" and guides decision-making to achieve desired outcomes.

Data analytics leverages various tools and technologies, including:

- Business Intelligence (BI) Tools: BI tools enable users to visualize and explore data through interactive dashboards, charts, and reports. These tools facilitate data exploration and aid in descriptive analytics.

- Machine Learning: Machine learning algorithms can process large datasets and identify patterns and correlations that may not be evident through traditional methods. Machine learning plays a pivotal role in predictive and prescriptive analytics.

- Data Mining: Data mining involves discovering patterns and relationships in large datasets through statistical and mathematical techniques. It is used to identify trends, clusters, and anomalies within the data.

- Natural Language Processing (NLP): NLP allows computers to understand, interpret, and generate human language. NLP is employed in sentiment analysis, chatbots, and text analytics.

Data analytics empowers organizations to optimize operations, enhance customer experiences, identify growth opportunities, and mitigate risks. It plays a crucial role in a wide range of industries, including finance, healthcare, marketing, and manufacturing.

In this chapter, we embark on a journey to understand the fundamentals of data analytics. By exploring the different types of analytics, methodologies, and tools, readers will gain insights into the power of data-driven decision-making in the dynamic landscape of the data gold rush. Join us as we uncover the transformative potential of data analytics and its profound impact on shaping the future of businesses and industries.

B. Types of Data Analytics (Descriptive, Predictive, Prescriptive)

In the data gold rush, data analytics plays a pivotal role in extracting valuable insights and unleashing the full potential of Big Data. Data analytics encompasses a spectrum of approaches that cater to different aspects of data exploration and decision-making. In this chapter, we delve into the three primary types of data analytics: descriptive, predictive, and prescriptive, each offering unique perspectives on data analysis.

- ❖ Descriptive Analytics: Descriptive analytics forms the foundation of data exploration, providing a retrospective view of past events and performance. This type of analytics aims to summarize historical data, identify trends, and present key performance indicators (KPIs) and metrics. By visualizing data through charts, graphs, and dashboards, descriptive analytics helps stakeholders understand what has happened in their business.

For example, in an e-commerce setting, descriptive analytics can present sales trends over time, highlight top-selling products, and provide insights into customer behavior and preferences. This historical overview is crucial for understanding past successes and challenges, informing decision-making for the future.

❖ Predictive Analytics: Predictive analytics takes data analysis to a more forward-looking perspective by forecasting future outcomes based on historical data. It employs statistical modeling, machine learning algorithms, and data mining techniques to identify patterns and relationships in the data.

Predictive analytics aims to answer the question "What is likely to happen?" By leveraging historical data and identifying trends, predictive models can make data-driven forecasts. For instance, in financial services, predictive analytics can be used to forecast stock market trends, assess credit risk, or predict customer churn. These insights enable organizations to proactively plan for the future and take preventive measures.

❖ Prescriptive Analytics: Prescriptive analytics goes beyond predicting future outcomes by recommending optimal actions to achieve specific objectives. It answers the question "What should we do?" and guides decision-making by providing actionable intelligence.

Prescriptive analytics employs advanced modeling techniques and optimization algorithms to identify the best course of action based on predictive insights and business constraints. For example, in supply chain management, prescriptive analytics can optimize inventory levels, delivery routes, and production schedules to minimize costs while meeting customer demand.

By combining descriptive, predictive, and prescriptive analytics, organizations can build a comprehensive data-driven approach to decision-making. Descriptive analytics provides a historical context, predictive analytics offers future foresight, and prescriptive analytics guides actionable strategies.

In the data gold rush era, data analytics has become an indispensable tool for organizations seeking to gain a competitive advantage. By understanding the different types of data analytics and their respective roles, readers will gain valuable insights into how to harness the power of data to drive success in "The Data Gold Rush." Join us on this enlightening journey as we explore the diverse facets of data analytics and its transformative impact on the dynamic world of data-driven decision-making.

C. Leveraging Analytics for Business Insights

In the data gold rush, data analytics has become a game-changer for organizations seeking to gain a competitive edge and drive data-driven decision-making. The ability to derive meaningful insights from data empowers businesses to understand customer behavior, optimize operations, and identify growth opportunities. In this chapter, we explore how organizations can leverage analytics to extract valuable business insights that lead to informed strategies and actionable outcomes.

❖ Customer Behavior Analysis: Data analytics allows organizations to gain deep insights into customer behavior and preferences. By analyzing historical transaction data, website interactions, and social media engagement, businesses can identify patterns, segment customers, and tailor personalized experiences. Understanding customer preferences enables targeted marketing, improved customer service, and increased customer loyalty.

❖ Market Trends and Competitor Analysis: Data analytics empowers organizations to stay ahead of market trends and monitor competitors' activities. By analyzing industry data, market reports, and social media sentiment, businesses can identify emerging trends and potential threats. Data-driven competitor analysis helps organizations refine their market positioning and capitalize on new opportunities.

❖ Operational Efficiency Optimization: Data analytics enables businesses to optimize their operational processes. By analyzing production data, supply chain metrics, and resource allocation, organizations can identify inefficiencies and bottlenecks. Data-driven insights facilitate process improvements, cost reduction, and enhanced productivity.

❖ Risk Assessment and Fraud Detection: Analytics plays a crucial role in risk assessment and fraud detection across industries. By leveraging historical data and machine learning algorithms, organizations can detect anomalies, identify potential fraud, and mitigate risks effectively. Data analytics helps financial institutions assess credit risk, insurance companies detect fraudulent claims, and cybersecurity teams identify unusual behavior.

❖ Product and Service Innovation: Data analytics drives product and service innovation by providing data-driven feedback. By analyzing customer feedback, user behavior, and market demand, organizations can identify opportunities for new product development and service enhancements. Data-driven innovation increases product success rates and customer satisfaction.

❖ Predictive Maintenance: In industries like manufacturing and transportation, predictive maintenance is a key application of data analytics. By analyzing machine sensor data, organizations can predict equipment failures and schedule maintenance proactively. This approach minimizes downtime, reduces maintenance costs, and extends asset lifespans.

❖ Supply Chain Optimization: Data analytics enables supply chain optimization by providing real-time visibility into inventory levels, demand forecasting, and supplier performance. By streamlining the supply chain, organizations can reduce lead times, minimize stockouts, and optimize inventory management.

❖ Real-Time Decision-Making: With the availability of real-time data analytics, organizations can make data-driven decisions on the fly. Real-time analytics empowers businesses to respond swiftly to changing market conditions, customer demands, and emerging opportunities.

To leverage analytics effectively, organizations must foster a data-driven culture, where data literacy and analytical skills are encouraged at all levels. Investing in data infrastructure, analytics tools, and talent is essential to building a successful data analytics capability.

In this chapter, we explore the transformative power of data analytics in generating valuable business insights. By harnessing the potential of analytics, readers will gain a deeper understanding of how data-driven decision-making fuels success in "The Data Gold Rush." Join us on this enlightening journey as we explore the diverse applications of data analytics and its profound impact on shaping the data-driven future of businesses and industries.

Chapter 6
The Alchemists: Data Scientists and Engineers

A. The Role of Data Scientists

In the data gold rush, data scientists have emerged as the modern-day alchemists, transforming raw data into valuable insights and knowledge. As organizations increasingly recognize the potential of Big Data, the role of data scientists has become crucial in deciphering the data's hidden treasures. In this chapter, we explore the multifaceted role of data scientists and the skills that make them indispensable assets in the world of data-driven decision-making.

❖ Data Exploration and Analysis: Data scientists are skilled in exploring and analyzing vast and complex datasets. They employ various statistical and machine learning techniques to uncover patterns, correlations, and trends within the data. By understanding the data landscape, data scientists can identify valuable business insights that drive informed strategies.

- ❖ Model Development and Machine Learning: Developing predictive and prescriptive models is a core responsibility of data scientists. They leverage machine learning algorithms to build models that forecast future outcomes and recommend optimal actions. These models empower organizations to make data-driven decisions and optimize their operations.

- ❖ Data Cleaning and Preprocessing: Raw data is often messy and contains inconsistencies and errors. Data scientists are proficient in cleaning and preprocessing data, ensuring that it is accurate, reliable, and ready for analysis. Data cleaning is a critical step in data analytics, as it impacts the quality and validity of the insights derived.

- ❖ Experimentation and A/B Testing: Data scientists design and conduct experiments, including A/B testing, to validate hypotheses and assess the impact of changes or interventions. Through experimentation, data scientists can determine the most effective strategies and optimizations.

❖ Data Visualization and Communication: Data scientists are adept at creating compelling data visualizations that convey complex information in a clear and understandable manner. Effective data visualization enables stakeholders to grasp insights quickly and aids in decision-making.

❖ Domain Knowledge and Business Understanding: Data scientists must possess domain knowledge and a deep understanding of the organization's business context. This expertise allows them to align data analytics with strategic goals, making the insights more relevant and actionable.

❖ Ethical Data Use: Data scientists play a crucial role in ensuring ethical data practices. They must respect data privacy, adhere to data protection regulations, and use data responsibly and ethically.

❖ Continuous Learning and Adaptability: In the rapidly evolving field of data science, continuous learning is essential. Data scientists must stay updated with the latest tools, techniques, and industry trends to remain effective in their roles.

Data scientists often work in cross-functional teams alongside data engineers, business analysts, and other stakeholders. Collaboration and effective communication are key to translating data insights into business actions and outcomes.

As data-driven decision-making becomes the norm, the demand for skilled data scientists continues to soar across industries. Organizations are increasingly relying on data scientists to uncover hidden value in their data, drive innovation, and stay ahead in the data gold rush.

In this chapter, we explore the indispensable role of data scientists as the alchemists of the data world. By understanding the diverse skills and expertise they bring to the table, readers will gain valuable insights into how data scientists contribute to the transformative power of data in "The Data Gold Rush." Join us on this enlightening journey as we delve into the realm of data scientists and engineers and their pivotal role in shaping the data-driven future of businesses and industries.

B. Data Engineering and Preparing for Analysis

In the data gold rush, data engineering plays a critical role in preparing the raw materials for data analysis, enabling data scientists to transform data into valuable insights. Data engineers are the architects of the data infrastructure, responsible for designing, building, and maintaining the pipelines that collect, store, and preprocess data. In this chapter, we explore the vital role of data engineering and the essential steps taken to prepare data for analysis.

❖ Data Collection and Integration: Data engineers are responsible for collecting data from various sources, such as databases, APIs, sensors, and web scraping. They design data integration processes that consolidate data from disparate sources into a centralized repository, enabling a comprehensive view of the organization's data.

❖ Data Transformation: Raw data is often unstructured and inconsistent, making it unsuitable for analysis. Data engineers perform data transformation tasks to clean, enrich, and reshape the data into a usable format. This process involves handling missing values, standardizing data types, and encoding categorical variables.

❖ Data Storage and Warehousing: Data engineers design and maintain data storage solutions, selecting appropriate databases and data warehouses that suit the organization's needs. They consider factors such as data volume, performance requirements, and scalability to ensure efficient data storage.

❖ Data Pipelines: Data engineers build data pipelines that automate the flow of data from its source to the destination. These pipelines facilitate real-time or batch data processing, ensuring that data is readily available for analysis by data scientists.

❖ Data Quality and Governance: Ensuring data quality is a crucial aspect of data engineering. Data engineers implement data quality checks to identify and address data anomalies, ensuring the accuracy and reliability of the data used for analysis. They also work in collaboration with data governance teams to establish data quality standards and enforce data policies.

❖ Scalability and Performance: As data volumes grow exponentially, data engineers must design systems that can handle big data efficiently. They implement distributed computing frameworks and database clustering to achieve scalability and performance in processing large datasets.

❖ Data Security: Data engineers play a key role in ensuring data security. They implement access controls, encryption, and other security measures to protect sensitive data from unauthorized access or breaches.

❖ Real-Time Data Streaming: In applications requiring real-time data analysis, data engineers design streaming pipelines that process data as it is generated. Real-time data streaming is vital for applications like fraud detection, IoT analytics, and personalized recommendations.

Data engineers work closely with data scientists to understand their data requirements and optimize the data pipeline for analysis. Collaboration between data engineers and data scientists is essential to ensure that data is prepared and available in a format that best suits the analysis needs.

In the dynamic world of data-driven decision-making, data engineering serves as the backbone that supports the transformation of data into valuable insights. Without efficient data engineering, the data gold rush would remain untapped potential.

In this chapter, we explore the indispensable role of data engineering and the critical steps taken to prepare data for analysis. By understanding the intricacies of data engineering, readers will gain valuable insights into how data scientists and engineers collaborate to harness the transformative power of data in "The Data Gold Rush." Join us on this enlightening journey as we delve into the realm of data engineering and its pivotal role in shaping the data-driven future of businesses and industries.

C. Bridging the Gap Between Data and Business

In the data gold rush, the collaboration between data scientists and data engineers becomes the alchemical process that bridges the gap between raw data and actionable business insights. The successful integration of data science and data engineering is vital in transforming data into valuable knowledge that drives data-driven decision-making. In this chapter, we explore how these alchemists work together to connect the dots between data and business, ultimately extracting the true value of data assets.

❖ Defining Business Objectives: The process of bridging the gap begins with a clear understanding of the organization's business objectives. Data scientists and engineers collaborate closely with business stakeholders to align data initiatives with strategic goals. Understanding the specific questions that need to be answered through data analysis is essential in defining the scope of the project.

- ❖ Data Collection and Preparation: Data engineers take the lead in collecting, integrating, and preparing the data. They ensure that data is accessible, cleaned, and transformed into a format suitable for analysis. Data scientists collaborate with data engineers to specify data requirements and validate the data's quality.

- ❖ Exploratory Data Analysis: Data scientists conduct exploratory data analysis to gain insights into the data and identify patterns, trends, and potential outliers. They work closely with data engineers to ensure the right data is available for analysis and to address any data quality issues that arise.

- ❖ Model Development and Validation: Data scientists develop predictive and prescriptive models to address the business objectives. These models are built using machine learning algorithms and statistical techniques. Data engineers support this process by providing the necessary data and optimizing data pipelines for model training.

❖ Communicating Insights to Stakeholders: Effective communication is vital in bridging the gap between data and business. Data scientists work closely with business stakeholders to convey complex data insights in a clear and understandable manner. Data visualization and storytelling techniques are employed to present findings that resonate with the audience.

❖ Iterative Process: Bridging the gap between data and business is often an iterative process. As new insights are discovered, data scientists and engineers collaborate to refine models, adjust data pipelines, and further align data analysis with business needs.

❖ Impact Assessment: The final step in bridging the gap is assessing the impact of data-driven insights on business outcomes. Data scientists and engineers work with business leaders to measure the effectiveness of data-driven decisions and identify areas for improvement.

Data scientists and engineers must foster a culture of collaboration and mutual understanding. Data scientists need to appreciate the complexity and challenges of data engineering, while data engineers must understand the context and objectives of data analysis. This synergy between data science and data engineering empowers organizations to harness the full potential of data in driving business success.

In the dynamic landscape of the data gold rush, bridging the gap between data and business is a transformative process that empowers organizations to make data-driven decisions with confidence. The seamless integration of data science and data engineering is the key to unlocking the hidden value of data assets and propelling businesses forward.

In this chapter, we explore the alchemical partnership between data scientists and engineers and how their collaboration bridges the gap between data and business. By understanding the interplay of data science and data engineering, readers will gain valuable insights into how the alchemists of the data world contribute to shaping the data-driven future in "The Data Gold Rush." Join us on this enlightening journey as we delve into the transformative power of data collaboration and its profound impact on businesses and industries.

Chapter 7
Prospecting for Success: Data-Driven Organizations

A. Building a Data-Driven Culture

In the data gold rush, the path to success lies in building a data-driven culture within organizations. A data-driven culture fosters a mindset where data is at the core of decision-making processes, and data insights are used to drive strategies, innovation, and performance. In this chapter, we explore the essential steps and principles of building a data-driven culture that unlocks the true potential of data and propels organizations towards success.

❖ Leadership Commitment: Building a data-driven culture starts at the top. Leadership commitment is essential to communicate the value of data-driven decision-making and set the tone for the organization. When leaders prioritize data and actively use data insights in their decision-making, it encourages others to do the same.

❖ Data Literacy: Promoting data literacy among employees is a fundamental aspect of a data-driven culture. Employees at all levels should have the ability to understand, interpret, and use data effectively. Data literacy empowers employees to leverage data in their roles and contributes to a more informed and innovative workforce.

❖ Data-Driven Decision-Making: Encouraging data-driven decision-making means making it a standard practice to rely on data insights in critical business choices. Organizations should establish processes that incorporate data analysis and validation as part of decision-making frameworks.

❖ Access to Data and Tools: To foster a data-driven culture, employees must have access to the right data and analytical tools. Data accessibility ensures that relevant insights are available to those who need them, enabling more data-driven actions.

❖ Training and Development: Providing training and development opportunities in data analytics and related technologies empowers employees to build their data skills. Continuous learning in data analysis tools and techniques encourages a data-driven mindset throughout the organization.

❖ Clear Communication of Data Insights: Effective communication of data insights is crucial for a data-driven culture. Data scientists and analysts should present findings in a way that is easily understandable and actionable for non-technical stakeholders.

❖ Embracing Experimentation: A data-driven culture encourages experimentation and risk-taking. Experimentation allows organizations to test hypotheses, validate assumptions, and make informed adjustments to strategies.

❖ Recognizing Data-Driven Contributions: Celebrating and recognizing data-driven contributions reinforces the importance of data within the organization. Recognizing employees who use data to drive positive outcomes encourages others to follow suit.

❖ Ethical Data Use: Data ethics should be ingrained in the data-driven culture. Organizations must prioritize data privacy, security, and compliance with data protection regulations to maintain trust with customers and stakeholders.

❖ Aligning Incentives: Aligning incentives with data-driven goals encourages employees to embrace data as a valuable asset. Performance evaluations and rewards can be tied to data-driven achievements.

Building a data-driven culture is an ongoing process that requires continuous reinforcement and adaptation. It is not just about implementing new technologies but also about instilling a data-driven mindset that permeates all aspects of the organization.

In this chapter, we explore the principles and strategies for building a data-driven culture that sets organizations on the path to success in "The Data Gold Rush." By understanding the core components of a data-driven culture, readers will gain valuable insights into how a data-driven approach can revolutionize decision-making and shape the future of businesses and industries. Join us on this enlightening journey as we delve into the transformative power of building a data-driven culture and its profound impact on the dynamic world of data-driven organizations.

B. Implementing Data Governance

In the data gold rush, data governance is the compass that guides organizations towards success by ensuring the proper management, availability, integrity, and security of data. Data governance is a framework of policies, processes, and controls that govern the entire data lifecycle, from data collection to analysis and decision-making. In this chapter, we explore the critical importance of implementing data governance and its role in building a robust and sustainable data-driven organization.

❖ Data Quality and Integrity: Data governance focuses on maintaining data quality and integrity throughout its journey. It establishes standards for data accuracy, completeness, and consistency. By implementing data governance practices, organizations can rely on trustworthy data insights to inform their strategies.

❖ Data Ownership and Accountability: Data governance assigns data ownership and accountability to individuals or teams within the organization. This clear ownership ensures that data-related decisions are made by the right stakeholders, facilitating better data management and utilization.

❖ Data Privacy and Compliance: In the age of increasing data privacy regulations, data governance is essential for ensuring compliance with data protection laws and industry standards. It establishes protocols for data anonymization, encryption, and access controls to protect sensitive information.

❖ Data Documentation: Data governance mandates the documentation of data assets, data dictionaries, and data lineage. Comprehensive documentation enhances data transparency, making it easier for users to understand data sources and make informed decisions.

❖ Data Security and Access Control: Data governance encompasses data security measures that safeguard data from unauthorized access, breaches, and cyber threats. Role-based access control ensures that only authorized users can access specific data.

❖ Data Retention and Archiving: Data governance establishes data retention policies to determine how long data should be stored and when it should be archived or deleted. This minimizes data clutter and ensures compliance with data regulations.

❖ Data Integration and Standardization: Data governance promotes data integration and standardization across different systems and departments. Standardized data formats and protocols facilitate seamless data exchange and enable a unified view of data.

❖ Data Governance Committee: Establishing a data governance committee with representatives from various departments ensures cross-functional collaboration in data governance efforts. The committee oversees data governance initiatives and makes decisions to align data governance with organizational objectives.

❖ Continuous Monitoring and Auditing: Data governance involves continuous monitoring and auditing of data processes and practices to identify and rectify any potential issues or gaps in data management. Regular audits ensure that data governance policies are followed consistently.

❖ Data Governance Maturity Model: Organizations can use a data governance maturity model to assess their data governance capabilities and plan for continuous improvement. The maturity model allows organizations to identify areas for enhancement and allocate resources effectively.

Implementing data governance is an ongoing process that requires commitment from leadership and the active participation of all stakeholders. It is a foundational element in building a data-driven organization that can harness the full potential of data in the data gold rush.

In this chapter, we explore the critical significance of implementing data governance and its role in shaping data-driven success in "The Data Gold Rush." By understanding the key principles and practices of data governance, readers will gain valuable insights into how data governance establishes the pillars of data integrity, security, and compliance that support data-driven decision-making. Join us on this enlightening journey as we delve into the transformative power of data governance and its profound impact on the dynamic world of data-driven organizations.

C. Overcoming Challenges and Roadblocks

In the data gold rush, the journey towards becoming a data-driven organization is not without its challenges and roadblocks. Implementing a data-driven culture and harnessing the full potential of data comes with its set of obstacles that organizations must overcome. In this chapter, we explore the common challenges faced and the strategies to navigate the roadblocks in the quest for data-driven success.

❖ Data Silos: One of the significant challenges organizations encounter is data silos, where data is stored and managed in isolated systems or departments. Data silos hinder data accessibility and integration, making it challenging to gain a comprehensive view of the organization's data. Breaking down data silos requires collaboration and a data governance framework that promotes data sharing across the organization.

❖ Data Quality and Trust: Data quality issues can undermine confidence in data-driven decision-making. Inaccurate or incomplete data can lead to erroneous insights and misguided strategies. Organizations must invest in data governance, data cleaning, and validation processes to ensure data quality and build trust in data analysis.

❖ Resistance to Change: Implementing a data-driven culture often faces resistance from employees who are accustomed to traditional decision-making processes. Overcoming resistance requires effective change management strategies, transparent communication, and showcasing the benefits of data-driven approaches.

❖ Lack of Data Literacy: Insufficient data literacy among employees is a roadblock to embracing data-driven practices. Organizations should invest in training and development programs to enhance data literacy skills across all levels of the workforce.

❖ Data Security and Privacy Concerns: With the increasing focus on data privacy and security, organizations must address concerns about data breaches and misuse. Robust data security measures, compliance with data protection regulations, and transparency about data practices can address these concerns.

❖ Limited Budget and Resources: Some organizations may face budget constraints and limited resources in their data-driven initiatives. Prioritizing data projects based on their potential impact and ROI is essential in optimizing resource allocation.

❖ Technical Infrastructure Challenges: Building and maintaining a robust data infrastructure can be complex and resource-intensive. Organizations must invest in scalable and reliable data storage, processing, and analytical tools to support data-driven endeavors.

❖ Aligning Business Objectives with Data Analysis: Aligning data analysis with specific business objectives can be challenging, especially when the business landscape is dynamic. Regular communication and feedback between data scientists, engineers, and business stakeholders are essential to ensure that data analysis remains focused on strategic goals.

❖ Overcoming Data Bias: Data bias, whether due to sample selection, data collection methods, or algorithmic biases, can lead to skewed insights and decisions. Organizations must actively address and mitigate data bias through rigorous data validation and algorithm fairness measures.

❖ Measuring Data-Driven Impact: Quantifying the impact of data-driven decisions can be a challenge, especially when the outcomes are not immediately evident. Defining key performance indicators (KPIs) and conducting impact assessments can help measure the success of data-driven initiatives.

While the journey to becoming a data-driven organization may present challenges, overcoming these roadblocks can lead to substantial rewards. Organizations that successfully navigate the challenges are empowered to make data-driven decisions, foster innovation, and gain a competitive advantage in the data gold rush.

In this chapter, we explore the common challenges and roadblocks faced by organizations striving to become data-driven. By understanding the strategies to overcome these obstacles, readers will gain valuable insights into how to navigate the path to data-driven success in "The Data Gold Rush." Join us on this enlightening journey as we explore the transformative power of overcoming challenges and the profound impact on shaping data-driven organizations in the dynamic world of data-driven decision-making.

Chapter 8
Ethics in the Data Gold Rush

A. Data Ethics and Responsible Data Use

In the data gold rush, the pursuit of data-driven success must be guided by a strong ethical compass. Data ethics plays a critical role in ensuring that organizations use data responsibly, transparently, and with respect for individuals' privacy and rights. As data becomes a valuable currency, the ethical use of data becomes paramount in building trust with customers, stakeholders, and the wider society. In this chapter, we explore the significance of data ethics and the principles of responsible data use in the dynamic world of the data-driven era.

❖ Transparency and Informed Consent: Organizations must be transparent about their data practices and obtain informed consent from individuals whose data they collect and process. Transparency builds trust with customers and stakeholders, ensuring that they are aware of how their data is used.

❖ Anonymization and Privacy Protection: Respecting individuals' privacy is fundamental in data ethics. Organizations should implement data anonymization techniques to protect personally identifiable information (PII) and prevent the identification of individuals through data analysis.

❖ Fairness and Avoiding Bias: Data analysis must be conducted with fairness and without perpetuating biases. Organizations should be cautious about using data that could lead to discriminatory outcomes, particularly in areas like hiring, lending, and decision-making that impact people's lives.

❖ Data Security and Protection: Safeguarding data against breaches and unauthorized access is a key aspect of data ethics. Organizations should invest in robust data security measures, encryption, and access controls to protect sensitive data.

❖ Respect for Intellectual Property: Organizations should respect intellectual property rights when using third-party data or sharing data with external partners. Unauthorized use of copyrighted material or data without proper licensing can lead to legal and ethical complications.

❖ Limiting Data Collection: Responsible data use involves collecting only the data that is necessary for a specific purpose. Minimizing data collection helps reduce the risk of data breaches and ensures that data is used only for legitimate and relevant reasons.

❖ Data Governance and Compliance: Implementing strong data governance practices and adhering to data protection regulations are integral to data ethics. Compliance with data laws such as GDPR (General Data Protection Regulation) and CCPA (California Consumer Privacy Act) demonstrates an organization's commitment to ethical data use.

❖ Data Use for Social Good: Data ethics encourages organizations to leverage data for the social good, such as supporting research, public health initiatives, and environmental conservation efforts. Responsible data use can contribute to positive societal impacts beyond business objectives.

❖ Continuous Ethical Evaluation: Data ethics is not a one-time consideration but an ongoing process. Organizations should continuously evaluate their data practices, policies, and technologies to ensure alignment with ethical principles and evolving regulations.

❖ Training and Ethical Awareness: Promoting ethical data use requires fostering a culture of ethical awareness within the organization. Training employees in data ethics and raising awareness of ethical dilemmas can help ensure that ethical considerations are integrated into daily data practices.

By adopting a data-driven approach that is grounded in ethical principles, organizations can build lasting relationships with their customers and stakeholders, earning their trust and loyalty. Responsible data use is not just a moral obligation but also a strategic imperative in the data gold rush.

In this chapter, we explore the significance of data ethics and the principles of responsible data use in "The Data

Gold Rush." By understanding the importance of data ethics, readers will gain valuable insights into how ethical data practices empower organizations to navigate the data-driven era with integrity and make a positive impact on society. Join us on this enlightening journey as we explore the transformative power of data ethics and its profound impact on shaping the ethical future of businesses and industries.

B. Navigating Legal and Regulatory Frameworks

In the data gold rush, navigating the complex landscape of legal and regulatory frameworks is vital for organizations seeking to maintain ethical and compliant data practices. As data becomes a valuable asset and the focus on data privacy and protection intensifies, organizations must stay abreast of evolving laws and regulations to ensure responsible data use. In this chapter, we explore the challenges and strategies of navigating legal and regulatory frameworks in the dynamic world of data-driven decision-making.

❖ Understanding Data Protection Laws: Data-driven organizations must have a comprehensive understanding of data protection laws applicable to their operations. Laws such as the GDPR, CCPA, and other regional or industry-specific regulations outline the rights of data subjects and the obligations of data controllers and processors.

❖ Data Mapping and Inventory: Conducting a data mapping exercise is essential to identify the types of data collected, processed, and stored within the organization. Maintaining an accurate data inventory helps organizations comply with data protection requirements and facilitates data subject requests.

❖ Consent Management: Organizations must implement robust consent management processes to obtain and manage consent from individuals for the processing of their data. Consent should be freely given, specific, informed, and easily revocable.

❖ Privacy Impact Assessments (PIA): Conducting Privacy Impact Assessments helps identify and mitigate potential risks to individuals' privacy resulting from data processing activities. PIAs enable organizations to make data protection a part of their decision-making processes.

* Cross-Border Data Transfers: Data-driven organizations operating globally must comply with regulations governing cross-border data transfers. Adequate safeguards, such as Standard Contractual Clauses or Binding Corporate Rules, may be necessary when transferring data to countries without an adequacy decision.

* Data Breach Response and Notification: Having a well-defined data breach response plan is crucial in minimizing the impact of security incidents. Organizations must promptly notify affected individuals and relevant authorities in the event of a data breach, as required by law.

* Data Subject Rights: Data subjects have rights regarding their personal data, including the right to access, rectify, erase, and object to data processing. Organizations must establish processes to handle

data subject requests effectively and within the required time frames.

❖ Employee Data Protection: Data-driven organizations should extend data protection principles to employee data. Proper data governance and safeguards should be in place to protect sensitive employee information.

❖ Regulatory Compliance Monitoring: Staying current with evolving data protection regulations requires ongoing monitoring and compliance efforts. Organizations should appoint Data Protection Officers (DPOs) or privacy officers to oversee compliance.

❖ Building a Culture of Compliance: Compliance with legal and regulatory frameworks must be ingrained in the organizational culture. Training employees on data protection and legal requirements fosters a culture of compliance.

Navigating legal and regulatory frameworks is a multifaceted task that requires collaboration between legal, compliance, and data teams. Organizations must proactively assess their data practices and adapt to changes in the regulatory landscape to maintain ethical and compliant data-driven decision-making.

In this chapter, we explore the challenges and strategies of navigating legal and regulatory frameworks in "The Data Gold Rush." By understanding the importance of compliance and legal considerations, readers will gain valuable insights into how organizations can navigate the complexities of data governance and ethical data practices. Join us on this enlightening journey as we explore the transformative power of navigating legal and regulatory frameworks and its profound impact on shaping data-driven organizations with integrity and accountability.

C. Ensuring Ethical Data Practices

In the data gold rush, ensuring ethical data practices is the bedrock upon which organizations build their data-driven success. Ethical data practices encompass a range of principles and guidelines that prioritize data privacy, transparency, fairness, and accountability. As data becomes a strategic asset, adhering to ethical data practices becomes imperative for organizations to build trust with customers, maintain regulatory compliance, and safeguard their reputation. In this chapter, we explore the essential elements of ensuring ethical data practices in the dynamic world of the data-driven era.

❖ Data Governance and Compliance: Establishing a robust data governance framework is fundamental to ensuring ethical data practices. Data governance outlines the policies, procedures, and responsibilities for data management, including data privacy, security, and compliance with relevant regulations.

❖ Data Ethics Training: Providing data ethics training to employees is vital to raise awareness of ethical dilemmas in data-driven decision-making. Training programs should cover topics such as data privacy, data security, bias mitigation, and responsible data use.

❖ Ethical Decision-Making Frameworks: Organizations should develop ethical decision-making frameworks to guide employees when faced with data-related dilemmas. These frameworks help employees weigh the ethical implications of their actions and make responsible choices.

❖ Fair and Transparent Data Collection: Data collection processes should be fair, transparent, and aligned with the purposes disclosed to data subjects. Organizations must provide clear information on data collection and processing in privacy notices or consent forms.

❖ Bias Mitigation in Data Analysis: Data analysis should incorporate measures to mitigate bias and avoid discriminatory outcomes. This involves scrutinizing data sources, using diverse datasets, and applying fairness-aware algorithms.

❖ Privacy by Design: Adopting a privacy-by-design approach ensures that data privacy and security are considered at the outset of any data-related project. This approach helps prevent privacy breaches and fosters trust with customers.

❖ Data Minimization: Organizations should practice data minimization, collecting only the minimum amount of data necessary to achieve specific objectives. Reducing data collection limits the potential risks associated with storing excessive or irrelevant data.

❖ Accountability and Transparency: Emphasizing accountability and transparency in data practices fosters a culture of responsibility within the organization. Accountability involves acknowledging and rectifying mistakes or breaches, while transparency builds trust with stakeholders.

❖ Ethical Review Boards: In certain cases, especially in research or sensitive data projects, organizations can establish ethical review boards to assess and approve data use for specific purposes. Ethical review boards ensure compliance with ethical guidelines and industry standards.

❖ Continuous Evaluation and Improvement: Ethical data practices require continuous evaluation and improvement. Organizations should regularly assess their data practices, solicit feedback from stakeholders, and make necessary enhancements to uphold ethical standards.

Ensuring ethical data practices is not just a moral imperative but also a strategic advantage in the data gold rush. Organizations that prioritize ethics in their data-driven endeavors are better equipped to navigate the complexities of the data landscape, build stronger relationships with customers, and maintain a competitive edge.

In this chapter, we explore the essential elements of ensuring ethical data practices in "The Data Gold Rush." By understanding the significance of ethical data practices, readers will gain valuable insights into how organizations can uphold ethical principles and foster a culture of responsible data use. Join us on this enlightening journey as we explore the transformative power of ethical data practices and its profound impact on shaping data-driven organizations with integrity and respect for individuals' rights and privacy.

Chapter 9
The Future of the Data Gold Rush

A. Emerging Trends in Big Data

As the data gold rush continues to evolve, new and exciting trends are shaping the future of big data. In this chapter, we explore the emerging trends that are revolutionizing the data landscape and paving the way for even greater opportunities in the data-driven era.

❖ Edge Computing and IoT Integration: Edge computing is gaining momentum as a game-changer in big data. By processing data closer to the source (such as IoT devices), edge computing reduces latency and bandwidth consumption, enabling real-time data analytics and decision-making. The integration of edge computing with the Internet of Things (IoT) opens up possibilities for smart cities, connected healthcare, and efficient industrial automation.

❖ AI-Powered Data Analytics: Artificial Intelligence (AI) is becoming increasingly intertwined with data analytics. AI-powered analytics offers advanced capabilities, such as natural language processing (NLP) for data queries, automated insights, and predictive modeling. AI-driven algorithms enhance data analysis accuracy and efficiency, uncovering hidden patterns and valuable insights.

❖ Quantum Computing: Quantum computing represents the next frontier in computing power. Its ability to process vast amounts of data simultaneously holds the potential to revolutionize big data analytics and cryptography. While still in its infancy, quantum computing's future implications for big data are promising.

❖ Data Democratization: The trend of data democratization aims to make data accessible to a broader audience within organizations. Through self-service analytics and data visualization tools, non-technical users can access and interpret data independently, enabling data-driven decision-making across all levels of the organization.

❖ Data Ethics and Responsible AI: As data becomes more integral to decision-making, the focus on data ethics and responsible AI continues to grow. Organizations are increasingly aware of the importance of building ethical algorithms, addressing bias, and ensuring transparent data practices to maintain public trust.

❖ Hybrid and Multi-Cloud Data Solutions: Big data storage and processing are transitioning toward hybrid and multi-cloud solutions. Combining on-premises infrastructure with cloud services offers scalability, flexibility, and cost optimization, while ensuring data security and compliance.

❖ Data Privacy and Regulation: The regulatory landscape around data privacy is evolving rapidly. Stricter data protection laws and consumer rights are shaping data practices and placing greater responsibility on organizations to secure and protect personal data.

❖ Real-Time Data Analytics: The demand for real-time data analytics is on the rise. Businesses seek instantaneous insights to respond to market trends, customer behavior, and operational changes promptly. Real-time data analytics is essential for dynamic decision-making and competitive advantage.

❖ Data Collaboration and Sharing: Data collaboration between organizations is becoming more prevalent. By securely sharing and aggregating data, businesses can gain deeper insights and drive collective innovation while respecting data privacy and compliance.

❖ Continuous Learning and AI Model Governance: AI models require continuous learning and governance to ensure their accuracy and fairness over time. AI model governance frameworks are emerging to monitor, validate, and update models as data and business conditions change.

The future of the data gold rush promises exciting possibilities and challenges. Embracing emerging trends in big data allows organizations to remain agile, innovative, and competitive in an increasingly data-driven world.

In this chapter, we explore the emerging trends that are shaping the future of big data in "The Data Gold Rush." By understanding these trends, readers will gain valuable insights into the transformative power of data and how organizations can stay ahead in the dynamic world of data-driven decision-making. Join us on this enlightening journey as we delve into the profound impact of emerging trends and the future possibilities they hold in the data gold rush.

B. The Role of Artificial Intelligence and Machine Learning

As the data gold rush continues to unfold, artificial intelligence (AI) and machine learning (ML) are taking center stage in revolutionizing data-driven decision-making. In this chapter, we explore the pivotal role of AI and ML in harnessing the full potential of big data and shaping the future of the data-driven era.

❖ Advanced Data Analysis: AI and ML empower organizations to conduct more sophisticated data analysis. Traditional methods are often limited by human capacity, but AI-driven algorithms can process vast datasets and identify complex patterns, correlations, and anomalies that may go unnoticed otherwise.

❖ Predictive Analytics: AI and ML models enable predictive analytics, helping organizations forecast future trends and outcomes based on historical data. Predictive models allow businesses to anticipate customer behavior, demand patterns, and market fluctuations, driving proactive decision-making.

❖ Personalization and Customer Experience: AI-driven personalization enhances the customer experience by tailoring products, services, and content to individual preferences. Recommendation engines, chatbots, and virtual assistants leverage ML to deliver personalized interactions that foster customer loyalty.

❖ Process Automation and Efficiency: AI and ML play a pivotal role in process automation, reducing manual intervention and streamlining operations. Robotic Process Automation (RPA) powered by AI optimizes repetitive tasks, freeing up human resources for higher-value activities.

❖ Natural Language Processing (NLP): NLP capabilities in AI enable machines to understand and interpret human language. This technology facilitates data queries, sentiment analysis, and language-based insights, making data analytics more accessible to non-technical users.

❖ Fraud Detection and Cybersecurity: AI and ML are transforming fraud detection and cybersecurity practices. ML algorithms can detect suspicious patterns and anomalies in real-time, enhancing data security and mitigating cyber threats.

❖ Autonomous Systems: The integration of AI and ML in autonomous systems is reshaping industries like autonomous vehicles, drones, and robotics. These systems use data analysis and ML algorithms to navigate their environments and make decisions without human intervention.

- ❖ Continuous Learning: AI and ML models continuously learn from new data, improving their accuracy and adaptability over time. This continuous learning allows organizations to stay agile in a dynamic data landscape.

- ❖ Healthcare and Precision Medicine: AI and ML are driving advancements in healthcare, enabling precision medicine, disease diagnosis, and drug development. ML models can analyze vast amounts of patient data to deliver personalized medical insights and treatment plans.

- ❖ Ethical AI Governance: The responsible deployment of AI and ML requires ethical AI governance. Organizations must establish guidelines to address bias, fairness, and transparency in AI models to ensure ethical data practices.

The role of AI and ML in the data gold rush is transforming industries, driving innovation, and unlocking new opportunities. Embracing AI-driven insights empowers organizations to make data-driven decisions with speed, accuracy, and impact.

In this chapter, we explore the pivotal role of AI and ML in shaping the future of the data gold rush in "The Data Gold Rush." By understanding the significance of AI and ML, readers will gain valuable insights into how these technologies are redefining data-driven decision-making and propelling organizations towards success in the dynamic world of big data. Join us on this enlightening journey as we delve into the profound impact of AI and ML and the transformative possibilities they hold in the data gold rush.

C. Forecasting the Next Wave of Data Opportunities

As the data gold rush charges forward, organizations are on the lookout for the next wave of data opportunities that will shape the future of the data-driven era. In this chapter, we explore the potential data trends and opportunities that are likely to emerge and propel businesses into new realms of success.

- ❖ Augmented Analytics: Augmented analytics is set to transform data analysis by integrating AI and ML into analytics platforms. This trend will enable business users to access automated insights, natural language interfaces, and AI-driven data storytelling, making data-driven decision-making more accessible and efficient.

- ❖ Data Monetization Ecosystems: With data becoming a valuable commodity, data monetization ecosystems are likely to emerge. Organizations will collaborate to share, sell, or exchange data securely, opening up new revenue streams and fostering innovation across industries.

- ❖ Sentiment Analysis and Emotional AI: Sentiment analysis and emotional AI will gain prominence in understanding customer emotions and preferences. Businesses will leverage these technologies to tailor marketing campaigns, enhance customer experiences, and gauge brand sentiment.

❖ Data-Centric Cybersecurity: As cyber threats continue to evolve, data-centric cybersecurity approaches will gain traction. This trend focuses on securing data at its core, safeguarding it with encryption and access controls to protect against data breaches.

❖ Data Privacy as a Competitive Differentiator: Data privacy will become a key differentiator for businesses, and customers will increasingly choose companies that prioritize their privacy rights. Organizations that uphold strict data privacy measures will gain a competitive edge.

❖ Quantum AI: The fusion of quantum computing and AI is set to revolutionize data processing and analysis. Quantum AI will enable more robust data modeling, optimization, and simulations, driving breakthroughs in scientific research and business applications.

❖ Hyper-Personalization: Hyper-personalization will take personalization to the next level, offering ultra-customized products, services, and content.

AI-driven insights and real-time data analysis will enable businesses to cater to individual preferences on a granular level.

❖ Data-Driven Sustainability: Organizations will increasingly adopt data-driven approaches to promote sustainability. Data analytics will help optimize energy consumption, reduce waste, and make eco-conscious decisions to support environmental goals.

❖ Real-Time Supply Chain Management: Real-time data analytics will revolutionize supply chain management. AI-driven insights will optimize inventory, predict demand, and enable adaptive supply chain strategies for improved efficiency and responsiveness.

❖ Data Collaboratives and Open Data Initiatives: Collaborative data initiatives and open data initiatives will gain momentum, facilitating the sharing of anonymized data across organizations and industries. These initiatives will accelerate research, innovation, and societal benefits.

❖ Data-Driven Healthcare Ecosystems: Data-driven healthcare ecosystems will integrate data from wearables, electronic health records, and genetic data to support personalized medicine, early disease detection, and improved patient outcomes.

The next wave of data opportunities presents immense potential for innovation, growth, and societal impact. Organizations that embrace these trends and harness the power of data-driven decision-making will position themselves as leaders in the data gold rush.

In this chapter, we explore the potential data trends and opportunities that forecast the future of the data gold rush in "The Data Gold Rush." By understanding these emerging opportunities, readers will gain valuable insights into the transformative power of data and how organizations can seize the possibilities that lie ahead in the dynamic world of data-driven decision-making. Join us on this enlightening journey as we delve into the profound impact of forecasting the next wave of data opportunities and the transformative possibilities they hold in the data gold rush.

Conclusion

A. Recapitulation of the Data Gold Rush

In the ever-evolving landscape of the data gold rush, we have embarked on a transformative journey exploring the vast potential of big data and its impact on the modern world. From the origins of the data gold rush to the emerging trends and future opportunities, we have delved into the intricate tapestry of data-driven decision-making. As we draw the curtains on this captivating exploration, let us recapitulate the key insights we have uncovered throughout this remarkable journey.

❖ The Value of Big Data: Big data is more than just a buzzword; it represents a valuable resource that organizations can leverage to gain actionable insights, drive innovation, and achieve a competitive advantage. The data gold rush has redefined the way businesses and industries harness the power of data to make informed decisions.

❖ Unlocking Data's Potential: Data has the potential to unlock valuable nuggets of information that can lead to groundbreaking discoveries, drive revenue growth, and transform industries. With the right data analysis techniques and technologies, organizations can unlock the hidden value within their data.

❖ Pioneers of the Data Gold Rush: We explored the pioneers who paved the way in data utilization, highlighting the successes and lessons learned from their endeavors. These visionaries demonstrated the transformative impact of data-driven decision-making and set the stage for the data gold rush.

❖ Understanding Big Data: The four V's of big data – Volume, Velocity, Variety, and Veracity – serve as pillars in comprehending the challenges and opportunities presented by vast and diverse data sets. Understanding these characteristics helps organizations effectively manage and derive value from big data.

❖ Data Analytics: Data analytics is the alchemist's tool that turns raw data into valuable insights. We explored various data analytics techniques, including descriptive, predictive, and prescriptive analytics, that enable organizations to make data-driven decisions with confidence.

❖ Data Science and Data Engineers: The alchemists of the data gold rush, data scientists, and data engineers play a pivotal role in unlocking the value of big data. They bridge the gap between raw data and meaningful insights, enabling organizations to make informed decisions and drive innovation.

❖ Building Data-Driven Organizations: We examined the essential components of building data-driven organizations, from fostering a data-driven culture to implementing effective data governance and data monetization strategies. Data-driven organizations are better equipped to thrive in the data gold rush.

❖ Ethical Data Practices: In the era of big data, ethics and responsible data use are paramount. Organizations must navigate legal and regulatory frameworks, uphold data privacy, and address bias to ensure ethical data practices and maintain public trust.

❖ Emerging Trends and Future Opportunities: The future of the data gold rush lies in the exciting trends of AI, ML, edge computing, quantum computing, and data democratization. These emerging trends present abundant opportunities for organizations to embrace and thrive in the data-driven era.

As we conclude our journey through the data gold rush, it is evident that data has transformed from a raw resource into a priceless asset, driving innovation, enhancing decision-making, and shaping the future of industries. Organizations that seize the opportunities presented by big data, adopt ethical data practices, and embrace emerging technologies will be at the forefront of the data-driven revolution.

The data gold rush is far from over, and its potential continues to expand as we delve deeper into the limitless possibilities of big data. By understanding the transformative power of data-driven decision-making, organizations can navigate this dynamic landscape and embark on a transformative journey to success.

In conclusion, "The Data Gold Rush: Unlocking the Value of Big Data" has provided a profound exploration of the impact of data in the modern era. Let us carry the insights garnered from this journey as we step confidently into the future, where data-driven decision-making will continue to revolutionize industries and drive us toward new horizons of innovation and progress.

B. The Lasting Impact of Big Data

As we reach the conclusion of "The Data Gold Rush: Unlocking the Value of Big Data," we are left in awe of the lasting impact that big data has had on the world. Throughout our exploration of this transformative era, we have witnessed how big data has reshaped industries, revolutionized decision-making, and brought about a new paradigm of possibilities. In this final chapter, we reflect on the enduring effects of big data and the far-reaching implications it holds for the future.

- ❖ Data-Driven Decision-Making: The influence of big data on decision-making is profound and enduring. Organizations now rely on data-driven insights to make informed choices, optimize processes, and identify growth opportunities. The integration of data analytics in decision-making is no longer a luxury but a necessity for staying competitive in a data-rich world.

- ❖ Precision and Personalization: Big data has paved the way for precision and personalization in various aspects of life. From personalized marketing campaigns to customized healthcare treatments, data-driven personalization enhances experiences, maximizes efficiency, and fosters stronger connections with customers.

- ❖ Business Transformation: The data gold rush has brought about a fundamental transformation in how businesses operate. Organizations that effectively leverage big data gain a competitive edge, redefine their strategies, and unlock new revenue streams. Big data has become a driving force for innovation and disruption across industries.

❖ Empowering Innovation: The availability of vast and diverse datasets has fueled innovation in science, technology, and research. Big data has accelerated breakthroughs in fields such as medicine, environmental conservation, artificial intelligence, and renewable energy, making the impossible seem achievable.

❖ Societal Impact: The lasting impact of big data extends beyond the business realm. Data-driven insights have the potential to address societal challenges, including healthcare disparities, urban planning, disaster response, and poverty alleviation. Big data is empowering governments and non-profit organizations to make data-backed decisions for the greater good.

❖ Continuous Evolution: Big data's impact is not static; it continues to evolve with the advent of emerging technologies and trends. As AI, ML, edge computing, and quantum computing advance, big data will push the boundaries of what is possible, leading to ever greater innovations and opportunities.

❖ Data Privacy and Ethics: The significance of data privacy and ethics has gained prominence alongside big data's growth. Organizations must prioritize responsible data use, implement stringent data privacy measures, and foster a culture of ethical data practices to maintain public trust.

❖ Data-Driven Talent: The data gold rush has given rise to a demand for data-driven talent. Data scientists, data engineers, and AI specialists are becoming essential members of organizations, driving data-centric innovation and decision-making.

❖ Democratization of Data: Big data has democratized access to information, allowing individuals and businesses of all sizes to harness data-driven insights. Data democratization enables data-driven decision-making across various organizational levels, fostering innovation and agility.

❖ Shaping the Future: The impact of big data on the present is merely a prelude to its role in shaping the future. As organizations continue to tap into the potential of big data, we can expect to witness unprecedented advancements, revolutionary breakthroughs, and a world that embraces data-driven opportunities.

In conclusion, the lasting impact of big data is an ever-unfolding narrative of transformation, innovation, and progress. "The Data Gold Rush: Unlocking the Value of Big Data" has been a gateway to understanding this remarkable era and the profound implications it holds for individuals, businesses, and society as a whole.

As we bid farewell to our exploration of the data gold rush, let us carry forward the understanding that data is more than just information; it is the key to unlocking a world of possibilities. The lasting impact of big data will continue to shape our future, redefine industries, and empower individuals and organizations to thrive in a data-driven world. Embracing the power of big data and the transformative possibilities it offers, we set forth on a journey of endless opportunities and innovation, driven by data, towards a brighter and data-rich future.

C. A Call to Embrace the Data Gold Rush

In the wake of "The Data Gold Rush: Unlocking the Value of Big Data," we find ourselves at a critical juncture in history where data is the new currency of success. The journey we embarked upon has illuminated the transformative power of big data and its profound impact on the world. As we conclude this enlightening exploration, we issue a resounding call to embrace the data gold rush with conviction, vision, and ethical responsibility.

❖ Embracing Innovation: The data gold rush presents an opportunity to embrace innovation and disrupt traditional paradigms. Organizations must foster a culture of innovation that values data-driven insights, encourages experimentation, and rewards creative thinking.

❖ A Shift in Mindset: Embracing the data gold rush demands a shift in mindset from intuition-based decision-making to evidence-based decision-making. Data-driven organizations prioritize data literacy and equip their workforce with the skills to harness data for growth.

❖ Navigating Complexity: The data gold rush is not without its challenges. Organizations must navigate the complexity of managing vast datasets, addressing data privacy concerns, and staying compliant with ever-changing regulations.

❖ Ethical Data Practices: As data becomes a powerful tool, organizations must uphold ethical data practices. Responsible data use, privacy protection, and addressing bias are essential components of ethical data stewardship.

❖ Collaboration and Data Sharing: The data gold rush invites collaboration and data sharing among organizations. Partnerships and data collaborations can unlock new insights and foster collective innovation for the greater good.

❖ Embracing Emerging Technologies: The future of the data gold rush lies in embracing emerging technologies such as AI, ML, edge computing, and quantum computing. Organizations must stay agile and adapt to technological advancements to remain competitive.

❖ Empowering Data Talent: Investing in data talent is crucial for the data gold rush's success. Nurturing data scientists, data engineers, and AI experts empowers organizations to make the most of their data assets.

❖ Driving Social Impact: The data gold rush offers the potential to drive positive social impact. Organizations can leverage data-driven insights to address societal challenges, promote sustainability, and contribute to the betterment of humanity.

❖ Building Data-Driven Leaders: Embracing the data gold rush requires visionary leadership that embraces data-driven decision-making. Data-driven leaders inspire and lead their organizations to new heights through the power of data.

❖ Embracing Change: The data gold rush is a transformative force that demands adaptability and openness to change. Organizations that embrace change and embrace data-driven opportunities will thrive in this dynamic era.

As we conclude our exploration of the data gold rush, we extend a call to action to individuals and organizations to embrace the transformative power of big data. Embrace the data gold rush as a catalyst for innovation, progress, and societal impact. Let us harness the potential of data to drive positive change, make informed decisions, and propel industries into the future.

The data gold rush is not a fleeting moment in time; it is an enduring movement that will continue to redefine how we live, work, and interact with the world around us. Embrace the data gold rush as a driving force for growth, prosperity, and positive change. By embracing the power of data and the opportunities it offers, we stand at the threshold of a new era where the possibilities are limitless.

In this concluding chapter, we issue a call to embrace the data gold rush with unwavering commitment and a vision for a data-driven future. As we move forward into the data-driven era, let us seize the transformative possibilities of big data and shape a world that harnesses data for the greater good. Embrace the data gold rush with courage, curiosity, and ethical responsibility, and together, we shall embark on a journey of endless innovation and progress in the dynamic and ever-evolving world of big data.